gul·ly

ROGER BONAIR-AGARD

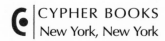

CYPHER BOOKS
New York, New York

cypher books
310 Bowery / New York, NY 10012
info@cypherbooks.org / www.cypherbooks.org

Grateful acknowledgment is made to the editors of the
following publications in which these poems appear,
sometimes in different versions:

Washington Square Review
Seneca Review
Louisville Review
Imaginative Writing, 3e
Union Square Magazine

Cover art: Steve Woods
Author photo: Rachel Eliza Griffiths
Interior and cover design: Tom Helleberg

ISBN: 978-0-9819131-5-5

Cataloging-in-publication data available from the Library of Congress.

First edition: 2010

Contents

Introduction

GULLY IS BEING PUBLISHED almost simultaneously in Britain and the USA, where Roger Bonair-Agard, once of Trinidad, now lives. In the case of the latter, he may just be a very hopeful and optimistic person. Perhaps he's received a revelation that one day the United States will become a hot bed of cricket, that because of the remarkable capacity Americans have of trying to rule in all things, it will decide to overwhelm the world with its prowess in this game. In that vision every American will know where silly mid-on stands, how a googly differs from a legbreak, or the kind of ball to play a square cut to. They will understand the functions of stumps and bails. They will know what a no-ball is, how many ways there are for a batsmen to get out, and they will not be puzzled by the prospect of playing a game for five days – one single game. Roger Bonair-Agard may have received this revelation or he may just have been drinking too much when he decided that the most fitting career move for him as a poet would be to write a collection fully committed to the theme of cricket (the sport, not the insect), and publish such a book with both US and British presses. Were he a more responsible and ambitious poet, he would have sharpened his Yankee voice, and written a collection about basketball. Heck, he could have even written a collection of poems about soccer – which might well become an American game. Or if his eyes had been on the British market, it might have been a collection of poems on running and jumping in time for the Cultural Olympics. But cricket? All this from a poet who, while being a Trinidadian to the core, has already been a national slam champion and established himself as one of the most dynamic spoken word artists in the USA. And whether cricket still has the same resonance as a metaphor for life as it once did in Britain – England at least – in the days of C.L.R. James and Neville Cardus, one must wonder. Well, whatever his reasons, he has done it. I think I know why he did it. He could not help himself. Anyone who grew up with cricket, and more importantly, anyone from the West Indies who was aware of the world in the 1970s and the 1980s, and who might have had an interest in playing cricket during his youth, has buried deep inside him an almost genetic connection to the game.

Like calypso or reggae, cricket, West Indies cricket, in the 1970s represents one of the most triumphant and defining aspects of life for anyone growing up at that time. The West Indies cricket team became the unquestioned champions of the world. They dominated. This is not an overstatement. They were ferocious, arrogant, confident, cool – and they barely lost a game because between the mid-1970s and the early 1990s the team constantly refreshed itself with good new players. It is hard to imagine this today. And even if we accept that a winning team can shape the mind of its fans for decades into adulthood, we should understand that these were no ordinary teams, and this sport was not just simply a sport. This was the sport brought to the West Indies by British colonizers. One of the pillars of the English cricket establishment, Sir Pelham Warner (himself Trinidadian born and a positive influence on West Indian cricket) came from a family that had been one of the earliest and longest lasting owners of slaves. Throughout the twentieth century, the subtext of world cricket was the dynamic of empire and the gradual collapsing of the dominance of the British in the world. In the 1930s and 40s, the West Indies had lived with the insult of being ridiculed as they competed with the dominant British and Australians. When they started to win in the late 1950s and 1960s, island after island was winning independence from the British. In the minds of many of us, the two things were not unconnected. The successful West Indian cricket teams of the 1960s were engaged in many evenhanded battles. Led by the supremely gentlemanly Frank Worrell, they played with much of the manner and politeness that the game had inculcated into them. Greatness and dominance were not flaunted. And if race was an issue (which it was – Frank Worrell was the first captain of the team who was not white) it was mostly understated.

The seventies changed all that. While Bob Marley sang, "Slave driver, the table is turned/ catch afire,/ you're gonna get burned," Clive Lloyd, a lanky, bespectacled, dark-skinned Guyanese was leading a band of dark-skinned men in a campaign of dominance that lasted for more than a decade. I grew up expecting the West Indies to win every time they played. I grew up never getting nervous when a game seemed close. They would pull it off. I grew up knowing that a rich and constant crop of amazingly fast and merciless fast bowlers was creating havoc and trepidation in the hearts of many cricketers. The confidence that these players brought to us made colonialism seem wholly redundant. It was an illusion, but it was a powerful illusion that made a reality of our conviction that we were part of a new and exciting generation who could be relevant and triumphant in the world. For people growing up in small islands with small populations, this promise of power was heady.

Which is why this book is important. It is why this book is important not just to those who know what cricket is, but to several other groups of people. It is a book about masculinity, about its evolving nature in the latter part of the twentieth century, about how men have had to be reminded of who they are and about how much they have had to adapt to meet the changes happening around them. It is about the art and psychology of playing a sport – how you learn a new language that becomes almost musical when you enter that place of heightened concentration, and you are reading the mind of the opposing player, you are calculating speed, and you are working out what your body is going to do and how well it will do it. It is about the dynamic relationship between the body and the mind especially in the unique arena of sports. It is about coming of age, learning how to lose, learning the pleasure of victory, fantasizing about greatness and then learning that for most of us such greatness will not come.

It is about ideas of home and the meaning of home to someone who has left home and returned and left again. It is about memory, the way we manipulate memory and the way memory manipulates us – the unreliability of memory and the urgent necessity of remembering. It is about being an immigrant, about trying to make sense of a new landscape, new language, new ways of seeing the world and contending with the world. *Gully* is about cricket, but it is also another kind of "gully", the "gully" of hip-hop, the place of ruggedness, toughness and the capacity to survive and thrive in dire situations. As you read these poems, you begin to recognize that this is not a study of cricket, but a study of how people grow up – how a man grows up in this world. And the result is a stunning and moving series of poems.

Roger Bonair-Agard's verse is marked by a clear conviction that the poem is rooted in the idea of story. But story for Bonair-Agard is not just a series of linked facts. It is the way he takes us there. I read these poems with excitement at the way he manages to find the precise language to capture something that seems immensely familiar. Here is how he describes the fielder, the gully of his title poem. The fielder in the gully is a close catcher in a position where the flying ball comes at him or her in the least predictable of ways in terms of height and speed. The gully fielder often has to bring off the impossible. Bonair-Agard catches all this in the kinetic force of the language he uses:

> I am trained to disappoint,
> my outstretched snatch of a one-hand
> catch must trap the batsman halfway
> up the pitch thinking he is on his way
> to more runs. In this position –
> so close, I could be quiet for hours;
> I could also be a god, a trickster god,
> a two-faced orisha, one who when prayed to
> delivers in the most excruciating manners.

Then here is how he describes the fantasy of a boy living out a cricket match – a test match, while actually in the rugged yard of his childhood. It is the dreaming that is beautifully captured here. Bonair-Agard captures the power of the West Indian cricketers' success in the world during those exciting days. That year in England, the team devastated the English team 5-0, a 'blackwash' as it was described by exultant West Indian fans. And the boy, Bonair, goes out to play a scratch game in his yard after the broadcast:

> It might be a six into Ms. Ivy's yard
> or a dramatic catch by the paw paw tree
> or the Bonair lad tearing up the pitch
> for a suicide single
> on the last ball
> of the last over of the day
> skating on the gravel
> the little white stones tumbling
> several over the other
> the whole cascade sounding
> amazingly like applause
>
> ("1975 – after the Broadcast")

And finally, Bonair-Agard manages to describe the "tao", the spiritual dimension of the game in the poem "New Ball". Here the focus is on the important rituals around the new ball in cricket. Indeed, oneof the things I have found most odd about American sports was the casual disposability of the ball. There is no issue with simply switching from one ball to the next in a football game, a basketball game or a baseball game. Not with cricket. The ball is treated with absolute reverence. The umpires are its custodians. They must ensure that a new ball is introduced after the proper number of overs. They must be careful, in the event of a lost ball, to replace it with a ball of equal wear and tear–as close as is possible. The umpire protects the ball. Every nick in a ball becomes monumental and can change the course of a game. Bowlers caress the ball, rub it against their crotch to make one side shine so the ball will swing. They drop it on rough patches of dirt to cause one side to be rougher so it will take the spin. Tampering with the ball is one of the most unsporting crimes in cricket–though it goes on! But, as Bonair Agard tells it, there is nothing as monumental as the introduction of the new ball in an extended test match. The entire game changes. Speed returns,danger returns, wickets fall or runs start to happen more quickly, and the game finds a new rhythm:

> I am a conjurer   I believe in ghosts
> When I am done you will believe
> in ghosts too
>
> My whole purpose   to make
> movement and pace out of thin air
> to hiss and spit off the pitch
> like a hydra

Here the new ball speaks. It tells you what it is, how powerful it can be. And Bonair-Agard does not try to explain everything, he just gives it voice. The result is emotionally affecting to the cricketer in me, but I also appreciate how he does it by the particularity of his use of detail and by the artfulness of his personification.

The danger of asking a rabid fan of cricket to write this introduction is that I become so fixated on the cricket of it and fail to point out what constitutes Bonair-Agard's remarkable trick of assuring the reader that the voice that speaks of this peculiar game is the same as the one that understands basketball and the streets of New York–the streets of Brooklyn–intimately and beautifully. The music of his lines is never as starkly impressive as in the poem "Goad":

> What bloodlet gang sign
> lets you be boy b-boy?
>
> what pachucho code? what khaki
> pressed clean into wheelchair ramp calls you home?
>
> what lover waits? what mother weeps?
> what hip-hop gives love and pours
> history's libation   for what stakes you this earth?

The pleasure of this collection is that as much as it is about cricket, cricket is, as he quotes C.L.R. James in his preface, not merely something that "reflects the age", but is, in fact, "the age", as are all "artistic and social events". James, the Marxist theoretician, the historian of Black struggle, and the novelist and playwright, found in his passion for cricket a perfect vehicle through which he could explore memory, politics, social identity and the complex passions of human experience. It is in his writing about cricket that James, the revolutionary who so admired Matthew Arnold, seemed most revealing about himself, about his contradictions and his passions. James gives Bonair-Agard permission to devote a full book of poems to the subject of cricket. When we read this collection, it is hard not to agree with James when he writes: "Cricket is as much part of the history as books written are part of the history". But Bonair-Agard has hit on something even closer to home than an effort to understand history. Cricket traces the contours of his emotional self and his understanding of personhood and, in his case, manhood.

There have been a number of Caribbean poets who have written about cricket in interesting ways. Most notable for me is Kamau Brathwaite, whose poem "Rites" (published in the *Arrivants*) remains one of the most evocative articulations of the relationship between cricket and history in West Indian society. But Brathwaite's work does not do the work of excavating cricket from the perspective of someone who played it, nor does he allow us into the psychological and deeply personal place of that relationship between sport and the personal. It is in this sense that *Gully* is an important and ground-breaking work.

But were the poems not so finely crafted, so brave, and so disarmingly honest, this achievement would be merely academic. What we have in *Gully* is a work that shows that Bonair-Agard has understood that poetry is fundamentally a performative medium. There is no great revelation here. However, when a poet understands that such performances happen as much on the page as they must on the stage, we know we are dealing with a remarkable craftsman. It is this understanding that allows us to celebrate this collection:

> I am a bird   my bird costume hangs
> in a window while I humor you
> in this mask of skin
>
> I am a bird sharecropping to regain
> my wings   The sun calls
> to me   It sounds like a grinding
> machine
>
> ("My dress hangs there")

KWAME DAWES
South Carolina

THE GREAT CRICKET WRITER, historian and statesman, C.L.R. James asserted that, "An artistic, a social event does not reflect the age. It is the age. Cricket, I want to say most clearly, is not an addition or a decoration or some specific unit that one adds to what really constitutes the history of a period. Cricket is as much part of the history as books written are part of the history."

That this might be so for the particular British time and circumstance that invented the game, and then exported it to its colonies, is only one wonder. Think then of the historical marvel it is to have had the game enter the conscience of nations oppressed by the British empire, then be among cricket's driving, identifying forces, and then imagine that those once so oppressed by the history that is the empire and its games, so master the master's tools that they dominate the sport for a long while – much to the chagrin of the commentators and pundits of that time.

Imagine the good fortune to be one of those subjects, to be Black and to have grown up during that time of black domination. Wherefore does a people for so long subjugated derive its identity, and how does it then learn to take that identity – hybrid and culled from various sources though it might be – and wear it like a badge? This is the story of these poems, and the story of cricket in the West Indies. It is just as it would be impossible to speak of the civil rights movement in America without devoting at least one chapter to the exploits of Muhammed Ali.

The rub, of course, is that the subject matter – or rather the vehicle for the subject matter – of these poems written while straddling the life left behind in the West Indies and the one embarked upon in the United States, may bear absolutely no relevance to the audiences that will hear/read them first. My hope is that this wrestling with the ideas and themes found in this game will be read as universal to all people – though perhaps particularly so to a people who are in an ever mutating search for an identity they can claim with pride.

Gully is a fielding position in the game of cricket. Close to the bat, just behind square of the pitch, the gully fielder completes the ring of fieldsmen that are wicketkeeper, first, second, and third slip, who stand behind the batsman. To field at gully (because it is close to the bat and because he is in a prime position for miss hit shots) the cricketer must be agile, fast, creative, either-handed in the catch, have a good eye, and great reflexes. Just where the elegant and powerful cut stroke is played, the gully fieldsman lurks. He lives to disappoint that shot, pounce on the mistake or cut off the possibility of runs.

But in the translation to the American Black English Vernacular, *gully* is also that deepest and most necessary of Black American mindsets – the need to stay *in the cut*, to get down and grimy in order to survive, because how else would one survive being of color in this time and place.

Recently, in a hip-hop culture tribute show on television, the honorees were asked what word or phrase coming out of hip-hop's culture of slang and language manipulation meant most to them. Various honorees answered in turn: *Fresh, On the ones and twos*, and to every one's consternation, *Beeyotch!* I asked a few other students of hip-hop and black diasporic culture who were watching the program with me what their favorite would be. In turn my friends responded with: *and it won't stop, grimy* and *ill*. A very New York, arguably even a specifically Bronx term, *gully* was my choice. For me it encapsulates the idea that one is "not to be fucked with", cagey, will do whatever is necessary, even including the illegal, to thrive.

It is the lot of the West Indian, the African American and perhaps of any peoples with a history of being oppressed. As such, it engages the translation of the immigrant poet from West Indian to West Indian/Black American. It acknowledges that in the cut are not just the boyhood heroes I remember and respect, but also a different sort of manhood struggle of which I am now also a part, and therefore calls on Barack Obama, Mos Def, Frida Kahlo, Emmet Till, Fred Hampton and L'il Wayne (amongst others) as mouthpieces. The choice of *gully* as a double-meaning title pays homage to this idea.

The game of cricket is a dramatic thing. At its highest levels, events in matches unfold over many days, over many meals and much drink with all the undertow of theatre: surprise, despair, jubilation, praise. It is my hope that these poems will encompass that broad sweep, and that something of beauty and sharing has been achieved.

ROGER BONAIR-AGARD
New York, 2008

prologue

Man-up!

*(a found poem—Principal Winston Douglas'
comments on the high school report card
of Roger Bonair-Agard circa 1984)*

It is a sin
against God, your parents and yourself
so to profane
the gift with which you were born . . .

Your responsibility is clear:
Be a man!

GULLY

1. a ditch or gutter
2. Cricket
   a. the position of a fielder between point and slips
   b. the fielder occupying this position

Gully

Here, ball comes off
the bat so fast it is sometimes
a flung streak of paint.
From here, how fast I am,
how snapdragon quick
my reflexes, can dictate a whole day's play.

A cocky batsman will cut
right past me – late or square –
and then I must become a bird,
a winged reptile uncoiled to snag
the catch so fast, the commentator fooled
already looking to the boundary
for the ball.

I am trained to disappoint,
my outstretched snatch of a one-hand
catch must trap the batsman halfway
up the pitch thinking he is on his way
to more runs. In this position –
so close, I could be quiet for hours;
I could also be a god, a trickster god,
a two-faced orisha, one who when prayed to
delivers in the most excruciating manners.

1978—London Street Arouca

We made her field gully
when we played on the streets
too narrow for any other placement
but one slip, a gully, a few offside positions
and a wicket keeper (for a right-handed batsman).

For a left hander it meant she was standing
in the concrete canal just below the level
of the street. I would cut to square—
the stroke I was only just learning—right
at the gully fielder. She would need
quick hands that close to the bat to fend
the ball away from her bony chest.
On the right she stood in the low brush
next to the bronken-down, abandoned
house where Angus used to live years before.

Neela was the only girl our age
who lived on the block—a shrill-
voiced, pockmarked-legs Indian
girl who cussed like a George Street
whore when we provoked her,
which was often, about her skinny legs
or any of the other crass things we had
learned to provoke girls about
in those scrambled pre-teen years.

In those days Lenny would come
out and sit on the steps of the abandoned
house to watch the boys play,
and he'd laugh at our hijinks,
his gold tooth catching sunshine
sometimes as he shouted encouragement.

It was Lenny who first called me
from the game to wonder about my batting
left-handed while I bowled right;
and together we sat for a minute
to talk about the other cricketers
we knew who did the same, while
Neela (the Indian girl with the pockmarked
legs) continued her scowl, her quick hands
making throws while her mouth
parroted obscenities at the other
giggling boys.

The only time we spoke normally
to each other was when no-one else
was there, and she called out to me passing
in the street or waved from her front
porch, and then she might smile
and I'd marvel that I could actually see
her teeth, which I remember as sparkling
white, though this might be how
my brain makes it up.

Lenny showed me how to skin
a manicou, after we caught one
sleeping in the zaboca tree and clubbed it
to death with a homemade cricket bat,
before we decided its meat was too tough
so we roasted useful pieces of it to feed
to the dogs.

It was Lenny who first said we should
leave the Indian girl alone and not
bother her so much. We were the ones
fretting her and I might have wondered
why she came out to play with us then,
if she didn't just like cussing at the top
of her lungs in the street, and Lenny
just said it wasn't right, so I tried
to be nicer to her because Lenny
was an adult who hadn't lied to me
yet, and besides I could change
anything I wanted.

What couldn't I do, who took
wickets with the right arm, batting
with the left, my favorite stroke a
square cut, right past gully?

and before the old black and white TV
is done clicking
I am already outside
mimicking the stroke play
of Viv Richards or Gordon Greenidge
or even more satisfying some days
Clive "The big Cat" Lloyd because he bat lefty
like me

and the hill of unused gravel
on my left was always
a badly placed silly mid-off
the smoldering dung heap
first and second slip   the razor grass
was a deep square leg
and the sorrel bush extra cover
and Dennis Lillee (it was always Lillee and Thompson
in those days) was coming off his long run-up
a menacingly tall mustachioed ghost
bringing the wrath of Down Under
with him – his white man's arrogance
the thiefing umpires
the snarling fans – everything

and the sun would be hot
and the shaved-down piece of wood
from Dolloway's lumber yard
would be my Slazenger bat
and the crowd would murmur
because the young lad Bonair
would step out of the crease
make the bowler halt his run-up

absent-mindedly pat an errant blade
of grass back into the turf
before resuming his stance
bat tapping too too patiently
like Kalicharran or Gomes
hint of a smile on his face
chewing his gum slowly – like Viv
a high backlift the way Geoff Boycott's
book said   and the delivery
would be short   a hostile ball
coming up toward the shoulder
so I had to turn on it sharply
left fist rolling over right wrist
so deftly the bat looked like a blade
flashing in the sugar-cane sun
and razor grass couldn't move
to the left   and hibiscus bush
just stood still and because
I was a cavalier stroke player
like Jeffrey Dujon or Lawrence Rowe
I didn't run – I didn't even
look at the flight of the ball
because I knew I didn't have to
and it was all the way down
to Ms. Thornhill's fence for four

In those days whole matches
were played by my hands alone
commentating in the public school drawl
of Henry Blofeld   and the insightful
Bajan twang of Tony Cozier

I memorized all the stats
kept the scores of a nightwatchman
batsman from day to the next
strategized on field placement
for the spin bowler and made sure
the West Indies always won
dramatically   on the fifth day
late in the evening
at the Queen's Park Oval
with rum flowing in the stands
a rhythm section gathering steam
and a conch shell fading

It might be a six into Ms. Ivy's yard
or a dramatic catch by the paw paw tree
or the Bonair lad tearing up the pitch
for a suicide single
on the last ball
of the last over   of the day
skating on the gravel
the little white stones tumbling
several over the other
the whole cascade sounding
amazingly like applause

at the top of the mark

and
        hot sun like blade
                  gurgle and pour
      rum
           half-past nine in the morning
cowbell   *cowbell*   *cowbell*
   and
       gleaming white shapes
             shift on grass

and

   BALL!
       red stain of speed   cow bell
           big spoon ringing on enamel
prayer
to pelau and slight pepper
                cowbell
         pull back and stroke
           mouth rich
     cloach   ball on willow
     cowbell   conch shell
   trickle and percuss
          hiss of rum in throat

and song and song and song and song
               and cowbell
and   crystal toast of glass
gold chain glint
   that sounds
  rattle and crisp
        of a good cussing

shuffle from the middle
the *thwip*   a thick top edge
the raw breath of   *howzat?!*
          cowbell

Mas' in the Queen's Park Oval

If you were a boy who dreamt at the lap of cricket's
 muse that year   your mouth filled
with the names of the British
 Botham, Gooch, Lamb, Gower
and you knew you were going to break
biche and head for the Oval –
despite your principal's most passionate exhortations
for the second One Day International vs England
at the Queen's Park Oval

Sun so hot only   the most intrepid will come
along that day   your friends not so much diligent
as unwilling to bake along with you in the top tier
of the schoolboy stands at the northern end

If you were lucky   then the man in the ticket booth
is your cousin-in-law's brother's friend who forgives
you all the $20 entrance so you and the only other two
boys who will say they were already too black
to worry about the sun making them blacker
will head for your seats   ticket clutched hard
knowing you have enough now for a few beers before 3pm
when you would have to head back to school
for your parents to pick you up
and act like you'd been there all day

If you had the good sense you skipped
early in the morning before
too many teachers saw
your face   If you believed in the gods
of cricket and calypso   then you were coming
with the hope that the West Indies would win
and did so looking good with delicate strokeplay
ferocious bowling and Gus Logie patrolling
the covers like a panther

and then you'd get to watch
what everyone had come to see   the world's best
batsman Isaac Vivian Anderson Richards
beat on the English bowling with such disdain
and smooth style you'd take off your shirt
in the stands   sing along with the other faithful
there who'd called in sick to work or had no job
who didn't care that the sun was hot
who brought their own
conch shells and tire irons
to make rhythm   said
Buy these young fellas a round
you'd turn on a radio just so you could
hear your own commentators florid descriptions
so you could hear Tony Cozier or Bernard Pantin
say *Another scintillating drive from Richards*
this is a boundary from the time it leaves the bat
Not a man on the field moves

You would join in and sing Blue Boy's
"Soca Baptist" and Rudder's "Calypso Music"
as the Viv – because by now he was the Viv –
smiled at every delivery he faced and made
all manner of inventive blackman saga-boy
stroke and he would twice in one over put Botham not just
over the fence but out of the ground altogether
and Botham could only shake his head and laugh
because they were friends and played for Somerset
together in the English County Championship
so they were still schoolboys together really
playing a game they loved
and so are you   but the game they are playing
makes you puff up your chest
because the West Indies can beat any team in the world

and it matters most when you can beat the English
with their clipped accents and their 3 o'clock tea
when you can go to the Oval   and truth be told
your prinicipal probably knows where you are
and doesn't mind as much as you think he does
because it is cricket   and it is cricket
to rally around Viv's exorbitant hooks and brilliant
late cuts and Holding's ridiculous pace
and Marshall's hostile rising bumpers
and you look around you
and marvel at a mad people
who celebrated everything
who brought picnic baskets full of pelau and rum
to the Oval   who were drunk even before the beginning
of the day's play   who didn't care how black
they were so they sat in the sun
without umbrellas   sang calypsos
to bottle and spoon rhythms
who made sure the schoolboys sitting around them were fed
throughout the day
who weren't yet noticing the dollar fall
or that oil money was done
or that Satellite TV and Video Music Box were coming –
or Germans would buy up all Tobago's beachfront –
who didn't yet know of a fall from grace
or that Brian Lara was yet to come
probably the best in the game ever
who probably broke biche that day too
but would be the only bright spot for two decades
and you wouldn't know yet of the cosmic
sense it made that crime would skyrocket
around the same time your boys would play
the worst cricket ever in their history
because Viv is driving at a rising delivery again

you see the shot coming because his timing
is impeccable   front foot to the pitch
wrist and shoulders following through
the ball whose pace and placement are so guided
by the gods of cricket and calypso
in whom you believe
that it rockets through extra cover for four
so fast that not a man on the field moves

Brisbane, 1975

(i) *Bowler – opening spell*

All morning, this blistering heat,
oppressive even for one
black as me, and accustomed
to Caribbean sun.

My tail is up, and even
off a short run-up, I am
a rainbow of fire and movement.

Still, not a wicket.
My in-swinger is hostile
and I haven't even rolled
my sleeves up yet.
The batsmen can't touch me.
I have them beaten – all ends up.

In the stands, the sea of faces
burned to a pink under their wide-brim hats
is quiet and confused, pretending
they haven't heard
a fine edge, or detected the trapped
stance in the thud of an L.B.W.

(ii) *Umpire*

I couldn't care less how much
this savage hoots and points his finger,
how many screamed *howzats?*
at what he thinks is an out.
If this boy thinks he will win
an appeal from me with anything
less than licking the stumps
clean out of the ground,
then this black fool
must be more stupid than I first thought

This is our game. We taught
these monkeys how to be dignified,
how to play the gentleman's sport,
how to be civilized. They'd still
be in trees if not for us.

Now they want to change the game,
embarrasing our batsmen,
coming to the wicket, top buttons
undone, trying to frighten us
with their shiny black chests.

I will show them. We are still
their patrons in this game.
Good white wickets are not
this nigger's for the taking.

(iii) Bowler – just before noon

So apparently, even an obvious
top edge is not enough
to give me my due.

I'm going back to the long run-up
To hell with strategy and field placement.
I'm not even looking for the L.B.W.
or the catch amongst the slips and gullies.

This next delivery will be pressure,
short-pitched
inswinger
from wide in the crease
up and in at the hapless right-hander
Let me show these fuckers
who is Man here.

If I can't get the wicket,
I'll take the white's boy's head.

dragon-slayer

We knew he was coming
he took his good and ready time
sauntered to the wicket
in the crispest flannels
a saga-boy lean to the walk

so man-beautiful women wept
openly before him   so savage
with the bat bowlers hung
their heads flabbergasted
when he was on the go

swaggered across the grounds
to what might be a slow hand
clap if he was at home   or a hush
if he was to explode
on a foreign theatre

arms windmilling slowly as he came
in   his desire to dominate palpable

Viv taught us how to walk
shoulders drawn back and always
smiling like he knew the secret
meaning of a song everyone
was humming

We learned to practice
our strokes and disdain even
to look at the flight of the ball
because like Viv we knew where
it had gone   nowhere
but flung like a rocket
to the boundary

Helmetless even to the most
hostile bowlers   we feared
and loved him the way
the village does the dragon-slayer
for the terrible deeds which
he has done and the knowledge
he carried in his armor

That bat we saw flash like blade
in the sun   when he hooked the rising
delivery   red leather of the ball
trailing off a swathe of blood
in its wake

And so we learned how not to fear
the crawl through John-John
or the worst areas of La Horqueta
how to fete with the Rastafarian
in Laventille and how to ask
a tall sister to dance

because we were mimicking Viv
the whole time   that steely nerve
the hawkish eye – that keening
ability to root out weakness
and exploit it

learning the way of men –
Viv's staring a bowler in the eye
from mid pitch before his innings
began a theatred devastation
of an opponent's will

We even stood like him
and learned to call out
all our names like the commentators
often did for him   so awesome
his aspect as he approached

Sir Issac Vivian Alexander Richards
we called out our own names
so Roger Anthony Bonair-Agard
coming out to bat   Cyril Elliot Smith
entering the cafeteria

Dexter Leslie Barrington coming
down the corridor   and we loved
the way our names sounded
in our mouths like that   how

we could make ourselves matter
even at our lowest points
like when Charles McIntosh died
or Richard Drayton lost his leg

Viv knew how to look good
returning to the pavilion
when he had made 291 at Lord's
or a duck   the ultimate knightly code

how to carve dignity
out of the nothing
of which we sometimes
believed we were made

earth and God

(for Hudley Vincent de Paul Bonair)

and now when I think of what else
my grandfather could have become
I do not consider his 30-odd shirt-jacs
in every pastel shade possible
lining the closet or the way his hat
fit meticulously at that angle on his head

or even that I held a straight razor
against his throat day after day
to shave him I was the only one
he let do it   or how he'd rolled
up his pants to show me how
the coffee was danced   or the years
of his turning the corner every Sunday morning
on the stroke of five past nine

lips moving silently mumbling the rosary
as he looked up to wave Sunday greetings
to Ms. Murray and Ms. Esme and Mr. Mora and
Ms. Alfonso   and though I laugh now
that had I known those shirt-jacs would be
in such fashion 20 years later I would
have snatched them right out of the closet
with his body still warm in the ground
and fixed them about my 14year old shoulders

And what I know   is that my grandfather
was the son of an African washerwoman and a French
land-owner   that he could have been all things
in a different world at a later time
had his skin not been so black-broiled
in the cocoa sun

And though I see his face quiet and unworried
as a baby's in my hand the skin pulled taut
as my hands learned latitude and nuance
the way I learned to windmill the razor
like Viv did his bat and scrape the grey hairs
off his face and against the soft hot cloth
I do not remember first that he'd been warning
my mother and me from months before
he even got sick that the land would be
in contention and that he wanted us to be sure
to get what was ours.

Here on the scrabble-grass edges of a worrisome
habit   when the bartender pours me the fourth shot
and marvels at my still lucidity and intelligent conversation
I do not remember first that my grandfather warned
that a visitor could never take just one drink
that the second was necessary to walk out
on two feet   this even as he was signing
his name to some momentously important
document in florid turn-of-century inkpot
British script   *Hudley Vincent de Paul Bonair*

And this is not a poem about cricket
except my grandfather was once young
and fast and black and when he was 80
I saw him wield a bat
with such fearsomeness   that we all
stopped our game and watched him
run and swing and swing again

and it's probably unimportant
that this was no game to him
chasing down the bigger boy
beating me up on the street
in the middle of the game
where my mouth had got me in trouble again

what I remember is
with what ease an 80 year old man swung
the well-hewn piece of willow

when he saw threat to his male heir
and I think about his perfect arm
action as he gathered speed   barefoot
on the road that day   on the balls
of his feet and breathing hard   how he picked
up the bat on the run and swung it like
the brushing cutlass through the canestalk
like the flat machete through the sweet cocoa-pod

and though this is not cricket
I remember how he moved like all the other heroes
we were mimicking that day
Gus Logie and Joel Garner
Clive Lloyd or Collis King
I do not immediately remember
how he taught me to discern Fever Grass from
Jerry toot bush or shadow bene from
useless weed struggling through the red dirt

What I remember first   is my grandfather running
impossibly fast and impossibly old carrying
my safety on the razor's edge of a bat
how he might have been so much else
but beautiful and reposed his leathered face
in my hands   he was every prayer
he needed to become   a man of earth
and God   and open-throat

Your fingers across the seams, short skip and a three step
run up to the wicket, break the wrist in toward the body.
Bowl a good length and the ball will turn away
from the right-handed batsman. Call this a googly

Run up to the wicket, break the wrist in toward the body.
Practice in your backyard against a wall or your motionless brother
a right-handed batsman. Call this a googly
and make sure you can turn it two times out of three before you try it for real

Practice in your backyard or against a wall
Don't let your friends see you labor this difficult ball for days
and make sure you can turn it two times out of three before you try it for real
Use it when not expected in a real match so the new movement is a surprise

Don't let your friends see you labor this difficult ball for days
You must look cool, like you master the swing just so
Use it when not expected in a real match so the movement is a surprise
and watch the batsman twine himself up trying to forward defensive

You must look cool, like you master the swing just so
like you and all not sure what the next ball will do
Watch the batsman twine himself up trying to forward defensive
and appeal anything that hits the pad for the LBW

Like you and all not sure what the next ball will do
and the batsman stalwart, patient, waiting for a bad ball
so you appeal anything that hits the pad for the LBW
and the sun hot and you done bowl six overs in all

The batsman stalwart, patient, waiting for a bad ball
so you roll up your sleeves and come around the wicket
The sun hot and you done bowl six overs in all
so you drop one short, batsman to the pitch, sweep, four more to the fence

You roll up your sleeves and come around the wicket
your whole line and length done change
you drop one short, batsman to the pitch, four more to the fence
your spell is done and not a wicket fall

Your whole line and length done change
Run up to the wicket, break the wrist in toward the body
your spell is done and not a wicket fall
Bowl a good length, the ball will turn away. Call this a googly.

New Ball

*the new ball must be issued at the beginning of an innings or,
after a specified number of overs of use, agreed upon by both
captains. At no time shall the number of overs be less than 75.*
(from *Lord's Laws of Cricket*)

I am a conjurer I believe in ghosts
When I am done you will believe
in ghosts too

My whole purpose to make
movement and pace out of thin air
to hiss and spit off the pitch
like a hydra

To be wielded in the hands
of men whose business
is carnage

To be faced by men
who are all fast twitch
hands and gladiator nerves

As the overs go by watch
them try to keep my shine
with a slow rubbing

a lamp lighter's care
for the genie inside
my high gloss and leather

a patient lover's compassionate
assist to arousal I leave
the perfume of my red streaks

wherever I am touched
Make placid wickets turncoat
with movement
Take care I am
a hot one and built
for nothing but speed and light

To devastate I want
to rear up in the hands
of a heartless man

one looking for payback
and shine in the employ
of fright and intimidation

I am looking for the motor
in my own stitching
for in swing and out

for the percussion of your stumps
for the soft cartilage
between your ribs

for the foolish edge of your bat
for your front foot turning
for your shoulder's terrified sockets

In the right hands
those of a man with something
to prove   I am looking

for the succor of your throat
the sweet hem of your jawline
shattering into the whitest light

Open Letter to Dave

We looked for you out the classroom window some days,
patient for your shuffle, the curved back
your leather slippers scuffling the pavement
giggling your way past our indulgent principal
(and your laugh as always made us tumble
out of our seats hysterical) your blue
polo shirt mocking the uniform
as you sauntered in always it seemed
an hour late for school

and for us in your bag
a bottle of Vat to take shots with
back of the room as we played cards
while teachers we couldn't take on
sallied forth and because we fancied
ourselves rogues we smacked the cards
down hard and called out Rummy
and downed the shot like hard-cases

and knew no trouble would come
because we had only weeks till graduation
and you had a game that evening

And in those days Dave, we loved you
because the strokes came so easy
because you'd made it to the West Indies
youth team and none of us could ever remember
you at bat without a smile on your face
like schoolboy bowlers didn't have what it took
to make you break a sweat and truth
be told they didn't We'd seen you break
a century in an afternoon with all manner
of left-handed flick-on and power-drive
We'd seen you decide to go to the wicket
with just quick runs in mind so you could

come back to the pavilion and drink with us
We'd seen you play internationals tipsy
and bat brilliantly We'd been guided down
Pasea Main Road to the dark canopy
of your father's rum shop to drink
and cuss quietly against the names of our own
fathers as we struggled with becoming men

So when I came back home expecting
you'd be moving up to the national team
and you showed up instead on crutches
nothing readied me for explanation
of our own dreams fading in the six
o'clock light of Woodbrook and the feeling
lost to your legs. Nothing readied me
for the idea that in you I was fallible
that I couldn't come home again not really
that we wouldn't live forever and
that your skip to the pitch the smashed 50
in twenty minutes so you could come back
and drink was a pinnacle come and gone
even though we were only twenty-one

And I didn't ask what we all wondered
– I am willing to wager – all alone and over
the next braggadocious shot of rum we took
whether all our drink somehow found its way
into the nerves spiking the fluid that ran
through the canals connecting your spine
to your brilliant brilliant legs the legs
that would run away to glory and take us
with them so that when we showed up
at the Oval we could say we know Dave
we drank rum with Dave in back of class
and Dave waited in the hot sun for us

with a bottle of Old Par perched
on a rickety table and sipping that
Dave was on my side in Lower Six
when we took on every other team
in the school on Friday and finished
Sixth Form unbeaten and made
all those other boys buy us beers
at the end of the day to boot

And in that wager Dave was a guilt
I couldn't shed no matter
how loudly we never mentioned it
no matter how easily you still laughed
even on crutches with the knightly lean
of the athletic hero

Truth is Dave I was angry
I felt cheated of your dreams
and wanted to tell you to stop
playing the fool and just pitch
the crutches away and start getting better
because what did I know about
desperation about needing enough
to be good at something before
everything you thought you'd
ever have might slip away so
when you asked suddenly
what I was doing in America
and I'd been busy putting up my soul
as collateral in bar fights and strange women's beds
your mannequin legs became an indictment
so in the panic I did what we'd learned
always to do I picked up a glass filled it
with rum and walked outside laughing
You'd already become easy with immobility

and you stayed inside chatting
with my mother while I got drunk
You had no interest in whatever neon-lit
promise the night's future held
for the rest of us so I took off my shirt
slid behind the wheel and gunned the engine
into the sparkling evening
and cursed your bastard legs a little
for your too soon growing up

To mimic magic

. . . To the umpires, he was malevolent stealth personified,
so they called him The Whispering Death.
                    −Wisden (on Michael Holding)

i The bowler is a shaman

Even on the black and white
we could tell the ball
was a wicked duppy

it moved furniture
spat and reared at the batsman's
throat shot past his chest
like a comet

the bowler a hypnotist
priest doling out a fiery eucharist
was all our fathers
a silent stern unsmiling man
nevertheless so smooth

we all imitated him
on the courtyard the field the pitch
especially next day

It was the fastest over ever

and none of the batsman's body
armor had prepared him for the placid
mat of a pitch suddenly turncoat
with grass and movement

We took turns practicing
the interminable run-up
the willow of a body gathering
speed and purpose like a train
head ever so slightly turning
side to side
the soft landing of the feet
ball cupped like a co-conspirator
in a bent wrist
each stride a human gazelle's

Dexter was the closest facsimile
we were 13 but he was already
six foot and slightly bearded
he alone had the body to mimic
the phantom ferocity the ninja-like
ability to approach in quiet and leave
a swathe of blood

but we all took turns anyway
giggling after each boy's gambit
and mocking excitedly the jack-in-the-box
twists the batsman needed
to avoid serious injury

Even then we knew we had witnessed
an improbable history
a black man billowing
like a sail in the distance
so fearsome that the batsman kept
his head down until the ship docked
a fierce unfurling of colors in the sun
and an explosion of gunfire
never heard before
We all saw it
We all knew it
but we never called it
by name

ii As for the batsman . . .

No slouch
his Fundamentals of Batting for Young Cricketers
was the best selling primer on the subject

Technically gifted
from foot-width to shoulder-placement
he spoke of the high backlift
against immeasurable pace
the low crouch to read
a devil of a googly emerging
like a rabbit from the hat
of a spinner's hand

He was an opener
dealt with the fastest bowlers
on the livest pitches
his history and authority secured
his defenses unassailable

but nothing prepared him that day
for the shiny new ball hissing
like a hot raindrop from the pitch

Twice in six balls his body
arched parentheses into the air
to avoid the missile
while the Bajans already drunk
on Mount Gay rum gasped audibly
at the spectacle

At home we inched our chairs
closer to the TV screen
as if we could shed all the fences
all the limits we didn't know
we had by bathing
in the ball's fiery flight

My mother avoided me
as one would a man
in rapt prayer the altar moving
with each spiteful delivery
and useless attempt at parry

iii Denoument

By the time Geoff Boycott's off stump
was dislodged on the over's last ball
and jettisoned 20 yards back
he was linked forever
with Michael Holding in cricket lore
in that way that history happens
in the past present future all at once
the way that real history
is poetry in the possible tense
the way all that happens is the rain
and none of us one man's house

We could not have known
even as we started
from the shadow of the West Building or pavilion
or wherever we gathered the next day
how much men and changed we were
school uniforms be damned
accelerating up to the wicket
in fascinated mimicry our flags
beginning to unfurl
our shirttails
blazing

dougla

The Indian was good
 we all concluded
and you would have bounced your head
if you thought you could knock him off
the ball Could screen like a drive-in cinema
and had a right foot like a cannon
Some days Shirvan could be dominant
enough at football that you forgot he was the most
exciting youth prospect West Indies cricket
had seen in years So imagine the lament
to show up to school one day to hear
the finest son of QRC blue had perished
in a car crash the night before the whole
yard a stunned silence

And for years we talked
about the squandered promise
of Shirvan Pragg boss batsman
but the Indian could kick ball too
we said and then we'd remark
how Dave was an Indian who
had a decent left foot and how
Ramesh could dribble like any
creole and there was not a hint
of irony in anything we said
reminding ourselves smartly
that Jeffrey's father Bobby Sookram
once captained the national team
so it wasn't so strange after all
that Pragg was not only good with bat
and off-spin or that Swami's flourish
with the bat was complemented with
a nice midfield touch We believed

we understood the places of things
and loved each other in such an anxious
proximity that we hardly noticed (though
this is a lie) the dougla children growing
like Ti Marie weeds amongst us

The Indian could play we said
and held him up like a bamboo-carried
puja flag Ramkeesoon or Ramnarine
Pragg or Sarwan we gave ground
to the assumption of cricket
or our own generous spirits in recognizing
their strength in football a game more
associated with our robust African comrades

We had not yet seen pace like fire
from an Indian had not yet seen
intimidation come from Bombay or Hyderabad
We knew only that we understood
the place of things where we fit
where they fit except for the million other
times we ignored what seethed
in our own good sense
our children morphing into brilliant
combines of the judgments we held fast to
while we marked their deaths

After the emancipation of African slaves, the British turned their attention to indentured labor from India to procure workers for an ailing sugar industry for which freed Africans refused to work, and starting in 1838, imported thouands of workers into the West Indies with false promises of earning wages to return home. Most often the terms of their contracts forced them to re-indenture themselves. They were brought primarily to Guyana and Trinidad.

I knew only that our three best
batsmen were gone
with one run on the board;
that the Indians were spinning miracles,
dervishes of doosra , and we were in trouble.

I knew our captain promoted himself
in the order to give them two
left-handers to deal with–himself and Gomes;
make them change their line.

I had always associated the stern
Guyanese captain with the great
Guyanese slave, Cuffy who rose
an army of slaves up in revolt
against the British. Lloyd did that
every year, but now Venkat and Bedi
were rising up too, and they were beautiful–
a Vishnu of arms, the ball appearing
and disappearing like prayer.

I did not understand why
the Indians in the stands were cheering.
They were all born here.
We were all black people,
so I could not understand their joy,
though of course, I could,
and it saddened me
so I concentrated on the beauty
of the brown men spinning,

my Cuffy captain's brilliant tactical
move, himself and the peyol boy
from Arima into bat—both left-handed
like me and patient like me. They defended
bat and pad close together, smothering
spin and pace alike till the danger was done;
and Lloyd would come down the pitch
put his hand on Gomes' shoulder
every few overs like a father,
and he was my father
that day I broke biche
by myself to go see cricket,
and they steadied the order,
and frustrated the Indian magic
and it was more than a day
before another wicket fell,
and the more they bat, the quieter
the Oval got until Lloyd would stamp
his authority with the occasional four
while Gomes contented himself with ekeing out
the intermittent single.

And I don't remember if we won
that Test, and it didn't matter as much
because it wasn't the English
or Australians of New Zealanders.
They were brothers there,
brown men googlying and off-spinning
their world into sense, except my brothers
around me, the Indians I walked with
didn't think so. They cast their lot
hard with India and for those series
against India or Pakistan, they spat
when they said Richards or Lloyd

and they made puja for the brilliant bat
of Sunil Gavaskar, and in my village
their prayer flowers came from my mother's
yard—the hiccupped beauty of buttercup yellows
and sultry hibiscus reds and they shared
kurma and roti with us and we lit
the deyas together every Divali
and Swami joined us for Christmas
and we raised ourselves on djembe
and sitar, curry and pelau
and nothing made sense that cricket series
though I put my head down,
practised my strokes in the backyard,
conflating Cuffy, Clive Lloyd and myself
in my own certain mind, shot after shot
bat and pad close together, forward defensive
left-handed.

gul•ly [*g u h l – e e*]

3. *Cricket*
   a. the position of a fielder between point and slips
   b. the fielder occupying this position
4. a large knife

we stay gully
    in the cut   quick-handed
  for snatching or the razor's
sweet edge

slip in and out   of shadow
    ghost   between
point and cover

deep
    like basement speakers
in summer's swallowed
low-ceilinged blackness

gully for blood
        and black
we stay
    underground
like that

The Gospel according to Trinity Street (Book 7)

Left a woman in a tie-dyed skirt
floor length hip high slit singing
a love song so sad she carried it
into churches and schools left it in
taxi cabs and other lovers' mouths
Woman sang so high so taut her dirge
became dirigible Funk so sweet
you have to leave a country to escape

She had legs like churches that she never
shaved and her belly button caved
caved like an intention toward
her spine Drove like a madman every
Saturday night I dropped her off
after the sweet funk fucking she put
all over my belly to get away from the
power of all that heavy all that heat

Nineteen and New Worlded there were
men with guns in their waists and bottles
of beer big as bazookas Trolled my way
to the courts where mythical four-finger
ringed figures holding up a skyline
on their knuckles laid down C-notes
on pick up games so I passed up
open shots and defended like a three-headed
junkyard dog Refused their ends but tossed
back their 40s night after night after night

When the magic devil's wife woman called
I was gone I was gone from under the safe
quilt she spun every Saturday night Funk
like a veil I was bulletproof I swear for at least
my first six months here and I figured out
the reason why – Check it

Every Saturday night before we hit
the party she'd make herself a new dress
She'd get down like the river queen and
exactly half hour later the humming and rattle
that was the machine or her throat but that
sounded like angels coming and coming
on some new ecstatic shit and out would
come something floor length like floodwater
slitted open to a hip like a cutlass swipe
meant for the throat and it was the throat
it throttled everytime She sewed in blues
and golds and yellows and bronzes the colors
of dreaming several cauls of protection and fear
and I would interpret these badly and grind
soft into the night with sometimes a moon
overhead and a soft surf trampling the night
a calypso in my unschooled chest
smelling the almond and cocoa off her warm
neck and unshaved legs till the sweet funk
of her fucked me down down into
a home would protect me but I drove away
from that   Two-fisted cutlass swinging
foot to the floor bareback and sweating
singing songs of love and triumph
lighthouses and seashells flowers and becoming

When she called I was gone
Her sobs were an open hymnal
for protection on the end of the phone line
the golden throat slit garments laid out
to make a sky for me but I was prodigal
I was already my own lament
growing callouses and scars into
one large allegory the surf could not unravel

Defense — 1988

Milt is chillin' / Gizmo's chillin
what more can i say, Top Billin' . . .
                                        Audio Two

I

pickup

The drug dealers wear brightly colored
velour sweatsuits open to the waist.
Thick gold rope chains hang
past their sternums Four-finger rings
mimick a skyline on their fingers
and the gazelles framing their faces
under the brooding eves of
kangols are epic They call me
youngblood or sometimes island
boy and they throw down bills
on the pick up games we run
under the lights at 116th street
My handle is decent   my passes
are money on a dime my J
is almost non-existent but my
hands   my hands are fast and I stay
on my man like a bad rash The first time
I hang out with the Kennys I'm scared
to play but do so anyway I am less
than a year removed from home
These dudes ain't no joke I'd better
play D Nobody on this court knows
how sweet I am with a ball at my feet
how round and rich
my baritone throat

cocaine

The two Kennys want me
to smoke crack with them
I won't so they're pissed
Still I pool my money with theirs
and in the back of an abandoned lot
in an abandoned car we take turns
letting a crack whore suck us off

I return twice more
to the lot once without the Kennys
and am a little relieved when I do not find
any of the dishelleved vacant-eyed women
walking around and willing to make
such an exchange

Later in a cramped bathroom
I will smack 200 dollars worth
of cocaine out of Kenny's hand
when he tries to force it
down my nose and he'll want to fight me
The close quarters are the proverbial
telephone booth in which I know
I will bloody Kenny's whole body
and for the first time I will fight
and not be afraid of whatever
United States Marines Kenny says
he used to belong to Fuck him
No-one in this bathroom knows
how sweet I am with a ball at my feet
how round and rich
my baritone throat

I've never told the truth
about this scar
its rough lip of skin
something like a history
on my right eyelid

So that my mother would not cry
I told her I got it
on the basketball court—a bracelet
or watch or ring coming down
to draw blood

So that I could call myself a man
I told my friends
the same lie and did not say
that my girlfriend imagining infidelity
and enraged swung a hairbrush at my face
which cut and bloodied my eye

did not say that in the next instant
I slapped her with a force that shook
the teeth in her head and that I slapped her again
and that it felt good which is to say
that violence does not emanate from us
but enters us in safe *justifiable* increments

In time I left before we could write
the end of a certain tragedy
The rest of the lie the one I am still telling
is that eventually the violence that enters us
leaves as unceremoniously as it came

The truth is that if you are lucky
you learn to manage it and speak
its name – speak it or have it
take center stage again when you can
least afford it and you must never think
yourself over the moment the person
the idea when its warm heft first slid
into your cupped hands made communion
of itself and ordained you
to a new more jealous God

American History looks for light

... Float like a butterfly, sting like a bee
the hands can't touch what the eyes can't see ...

Muhammed Ali

(i) the bullet speaks of purpose

Trajectory is everything
the difference between a kiss off
the ribcage or the blessed blood
of a ripe organ The brain
protests the most neurons
firing over and around the holy
landing trying to make sense
of it the wailing and the vivid
snapshots metal tendrils reaching
trying to block out the light

(ii) Malcolm pulls Obama's coat

there is no doubt
in my mind they will come for you
dozens at a time
miniature fighter planes built
for such an idealism as yours
They are amazing fish
fanning their steel gills
like razors
formations neat and orderly as a school
barreling toward the abdomen
heart spleen kidney anywhere
there is light

(iii) Obama plays the dozens

I'm so fast I'll be gone by trigger time
I'm so bad I beat Hillary by 30
I'm so slick not even Bill could sink me
I'm so badass my name is Barack
I'm so chameleon my name is Hussein
I'm so pretty your Mama canvassed for me
I'm so pretty your Mama voted for me
I'm so pretty your Mama is my Mama
I'm so good I shook up the world
I'm so fast I dodged a circus of bullets
I'm so fast I flick the switch and be in bed
    before the light comes off

(iv) the bullet takes the bait

Neither disease nor plane crash
not knife or hurricane or freak accident
is as dramatic as me
See the body begin decompose
in an instant See the body
become particular See
the body become tendrils
of impressionist thought See how
marvellous my entrances
how devastating my exit wounds
I save my best work for the stage.

(v) Bruce Lee knows from bullets

See this fist
this quick a capella kick
kung fu   sho nuff
what   see this
sidestep Tae Kwon Don't
you never think steel is hard
as bone – Barack I legacy you
Me – every dragon flow
strict mantis pose
struck to cobra swift release

Don't think steel is hard like home
See this river flow   bones
see how bullets bury
what they can't kill
See how I live
ecstatic – fly jumpsuit
dramatic – Barack I legacy you
Me – like I loaned Muhammed
the butterfly and the bee   we stay
vested – historically protected B
We battle terrific   Fuck Chuck Norris
me and Jim Kelly's got your hood
and your dome Don't you never
think steel be hard like stone

allegory of the black man at work in a synagogue

My name is Roger Anthony Bonair-Agard
My name is a myth of its own creation
its syllables conjured by fear
My name is given me by an anxious history
The meat of it is always about loss
and return
I was born
between two rivers
in a valley
of a shadow of blackness

My name means Famous Spear It is old
German It is the purview of warriors
My name means Priceless It is old
Latin It is the purview of kings
My name means Beautiful One It is old
French I wear it like a sixth finger

When I was 23 I managed the records
of membership and death   Membership
and death bear their own names
They keep mine locked in the safe
of their own mythology The old man says
Fuck You I say *My name means free*
to go about my own business

They came to me with solemn voices
to purchase plots
to give them seats in the temple
They did not recognize my name
Are you French
Are you a Jew Are you Black
May I speak to someone white

They came to me with celebration
This is my son David
This is my daughter Rebecca
This is their child Noah
Rosenbaum Miller Tisch Mandel
They brought me their tithings
of laughter history wine   hubris hate
I gathered them onto me
to make myself new armor

My name is the first born son
of a single mother   She is always
a basket on a river She is named
after a beautiful boy
Her name is the purview
of gods She holds onto me like a promise
She gave me literature and the love
of all things holy And rum is holy
and dominoes are holy and the smell
of night-blooming jasmine is holy
She adorns her walls with the crawl
of bougainvillea and these too are holy

During the High Holy days they come
to me for seats in the temple They come
to me without knowing my name They come
to me without knowing the meanings
of likeness and image But they offer me
bottles of wine and
They do not speak to me if I do not
have a name tag They do not
look long enough to see the name tag
My name means invisible It does not belong
to me My name means holder of seats
which are closest to God My name means
holder of land which is closest to death

I am 23 years old I am a litany
of violence I am moon
on a dancefloor I am drunken
promise behind the wheel of a car
They advise me like their own
son They urge me back to school
they urge me back into the carapace
of my own mind My name means
Guardian It is old Norman French
It is the purview of Lords My name
means elaborate caskets and endowments
for the temple

I am 26 years old I do not know
my name I am untethered as a cloud
They come to me with new ways
to talk about race They come to me
with words and new literatures
My mother's name means music
means builder of things She gave
me fists and a fencer's tongue
My name means builder of things
They come to me with poetry
It is the purview of the lost Thank God
they have come My name means
hunger My body means Hunger
I am a litany of Hunger
All these poems   Hunger

contradiction

(a ghazal for L'il Wayne)

Do I contradict myself?
Very well then I contradict myself,
(I am large, I contain multitudes.)
                    Walt Whitman

America don't want
too many layered niggahs

America scared
of another player niggah

You show America
how Katrina played a niggah

You rock and roll
vicious but still stay a niggah

You rep Blood ties
like you they mayor niggah

You spit grimy
flows like you ain't fraid of niggahs

Work for your bling
like a John Henry niggah

They don't know your
dark or how you heavy niggah

Can't tell you how
you got your pennies niggah

Tupac incarnate
You contain many niggahs

Show mad love
but take on any niggah

Stay lifted and tight
you rhyme with any niggah

How we gonna front
on an inventive niggah?

Wayne you are America
You contain many niggahs!

Andrew Jackson's statue —
French Quarter, New Orleans 2006

(after Patricia Smith and Kevin Coval)

you Indian Killer
you nigger-hunter and 20 dollar bill interloper

you chase Seminoles into Everglades
you westward expander and manifest destiny
you hunk of stone like a mockery
   in America's largest black city

you cause Katrina motherfucker
you park dweller reminder of pain
   that's why pigeons shit on your head

Jackson
you confederacy foundation
you basis for the KKK and buffalo hunts
you killed Emmitt Till and Yusef Hawkins
you tame horses
   and build reservations
      you small pox blanket and   Wall Street

you search for Weapons of Mass Destruction
you are Weapon of Mass Destruction
you Tuskegee experimenter

you boot-spur wearer
you fuck up only chance we had at bringing poor people together

you threaten poor white folk
  and give them money to kill others
Wait you George W. Bush

you big forehead – bushy eyebrows
you ultimate white-boy warmonger
you Bay of Pigs you Louisiana Purchase

and that's why we hip-hop
   and blues
that's why we represent
   and keep it real
that's why we tag your ass
with bubble letters that say
wild Style

that's why we black
   and light-skinned-ed

that's why we flag burners
   and draft dodgers
that's why we call ourselves Africa
   and turn to Islam
that's why we Crip
   and Norteno

you flight 93   you assassination bullet
you Gaza Strip and Kissinger's legacy

you plutonium enrichment
   and regime destabilizer

Jackson you
   fuckin' up my vacation

have you always been built of such calm?
how can the fire singe such stone?

Hymn

We buffalo up the bar like wild meat. We hold up ceilings. We steel beams.
Scaffold me a tomorrow, a son, and see what whiskers explode onto his face –
a promise. We light up most things. Rooms included. Wombs. Yes, we light up
wombs. Tomorrow a man with a mask is coming. Fuck him. Fuck his plans for
destruction. Do you see how we marathon ready? Do you see the quilt we
build steady? Do you see our rock ready for launching? We Broadway and the
Serengeti. We canyoned up hills and erected valleys. Imagine that. Imagine all
these people we love us ourselves to hold us together. Who think they breach that
wall? Who think they Trojaned a horse enough to not die trying? We Kikuyu
and Seminole in the night, just like that. Don't even look for us behind the next
embankment. There is a sword in my hand. I mean to use it good.

Goad

ode to colored boys

what bloodlet got cut gang sign
lets you be boy b-boy?

what pachucho code? what khaki
pressed clean into wheelchair ramp calls you home?

what lover waits? what mother weeps?
what hip-hop gives love and pours
libation for what stakes you this earth?

what invisible hate cuts you quick?

what slick move gun-slide
is your middle name?

what dance what flip what fist-first
policy in a fight?

what graffiti'd wall is your history's scripture?

what red what blue what sign what fuck
what wet-faced baby what baby baby please
what please God not my baby

what pretty face hot pussy like salvation

what war what turf what hunger
what father's immigrant flag haunts you?

what food what bird what God what ghost
what flight what flow what fantasy
of finally being a man
goads you to this fire?

i have decided to want . . .

to sing like my grandmother
in church before the fourth stroke
when i tried to match her
note by note

a child whose mother I'll have
to call and say *look what your child did*

babies   twins
a stoic boy and an impossible girl
to not understand my daughter's
endless breath her bright clothes

azaleas because I like how they sound
in my throat

a woman to doubt me.

I've decided to want back the small village
the barrells we rolled into the lot to play cricket
the sound of the leather on bat

my grandmother's wail calling calling
me home

I want back her laughter
that last time when she said
make me laugh again
and I did   even though i was 22
and felt a little stupid doing the old
impressions of my teachers and
Miss Lukus Babb
and Miss Mavis who was always minding
people's business

I want back the first time
I cupped a girl's breast in my hand
and there was the perfect roundness
its exorbitant give

I have decided to want a house on stilts

I want the smell of jasmine all the time
I do not know when I started wanting
the smell of flowers everywhere

I want to crash into things again
my body to unfold from angle
to angle to emerge bloody
I want to play in a yard
pretend I am the whole game
and all the players

I want the red dirt's fine dusting
over the shadow bene and the sorrell
I want the lime tree to be the boundary again

I want hibiscus bushes to suck
the sweet juice again from the flowers'
long stamens

I want that moment
when i learned to turn
the ball in one motion
from the outside of my foot in
the spanner   we called it

I want to practice it every free period
and recess and lunch
for a whole week I want
the courtyard's roar the first time
I put it on a defender again

I have decided to want sunshine
the slate gray
of an overcast sky and a child
who rolls
her eyes when i speak

another who paints and hardly speaks
except for when his spanner is deadly
with either foot

My dress hangs there

(after Frida Kahlo)

I am a bird   my bird costume hangs
in a window while I humor you
in this mask of skin

I am a bird sharecropping to regain
my wings   The sun calls
to me   It sounds like a grinding
machine

I am a bird something full of sex
and allure like an eagle
like a mallard like a vulture

I am a bird Your promises continue
to pluck at my feathers I molt
because of your concrete and steel
dreams

Look at my skeleton walking
about you You always pretend
this is skin I am a bird dying
without a sky for a grave
You hold my wings as collateral
My ghost prepares to haunt your
dusty attic

a scattering of bones

we are a balance of bones
thrown one way for divination
the next for warfare
Each morning brings us a sun
of our own making the froth
of all our angers   all our hesitations
combined   Every morning I climb
an unknown parapet to fire a flare
into the black This is before daybreak
before things have names before
anyone or animal with a mandate
can call out to its god   call out
to another day to make form out
of what is simple light   Some
break the dried coconut and ask
its random leaves for the answer
We speak through its several shards
It is how we make a way
out of what might be merely
chance   In the early shine
bones names heat thought
all take specific form to us We
make worship of these new shapes
We are sure of this day
We have learned to call them by name

burial instructions for the lovely death

(after Lynne Procope)

Tag up the pine box
in the handiwork of children

Let them beat on biscuit tins
with sticks and lengths of pipe
till every ding and dent
is an electric resonance

Remind the congregation
of my every transgression
the woman I told I'd wait
forever   how I did not honor
my mother and became the most
inadequate version of my father

Pick the flowers by hand
Steal them from public gardens
Bring them root-bleeding to the burial
ground and toss them all atop
the coffin like a blazing pyre of color
Say *hydrangea*   Say *azalea*
Say *rose* and *jasmine*
Say *buttercup* and *chrysanthemum*
Say *lily* and *orchid* and *sunflower*
Let all the bass voices whisper
jonquil in its inevitable blue

Because the death will be a spectacle
of pain and undignified screaming
let the party go graveside throughout
the night – fanfare of horn in service
of salsa and kaiso – the one drop kick
snare of reggae and hip-hop over
the rumbling throat-raw vocals of whores

Let there be cussing and a deluge
of rum poured on the burial mound
so that the dirt be packed tight a match
lit to it and burned to a pyre of exult
Let all without faith or hope warm themselves
in this unholy heat – Fuck my poems
Critique them mercilessly in the light there
Feed the fire on my bones and the fists
they still mimic   Let me be useful
in my final moments   splintered kindling
a symbol of what I wanted to be
before I learned to spell failure in my
own flesh molting into earth

the tragicomedy of the black boy blues
or a hip-hop nigretto
or the boy became black at JFK

Is the boy with the umbrella worried
who will protect him next?
is his skin the color of his true
love's hair? are umbrellas totems or buildings?

Is green a color or an emotive state?
are the boys running behind the black boy
laughing or just baring their teeth? is it any
different whether they spit on him or soak
him in gasoline? Say wither. Say the bathwater
went out with the baby. Say the baby.
Say the Germans had to have had something right
wing. Say we're all just billboards anyway.

There is something absolutely fearless
about leaving your house in the world
and going abroad when you are black
and ruled by nothing but fast twitch
fibers and the fear of standing still When
the instinct is all feint and dip sharp
left jab-step and full sprint right
split knuckle and the rust of blood in the cheek.

If we are all to be truthful
we're pretty sure the girl wants nothing
to do with us but the black boy
does. If we are all to be truthful we
can already smell his black flesh
burning. Can't you hear it? the crackled
skin? the smell of pork rind in the air?
the eyeball pop? the drop-step rhythm
dissipate with the rope fibers in
the morning air? Aren't we all just
standing around watching things fall
from the sky or burn into the ether?

Where do black boys go when they
fail? Where do black boys go when
they succeed? Where do black boys go
when they die; when the skin is ashes
to dust? Where do black boys go
when they feel the need to scale fences?

You can only move as fast as who's
in front of you – that's what the black boy
says – unless you carefully slit the
Achilles tendon of a muthafucka and let
him bleed to a halt. This is the leapfrog
dance and this is America. black boys
waiting. black boys waiting.
What happens to a black boy if he just
stands still?

and three times we made love on
the banister of her father's condo and three
times she told me she loved me and
three times she emphasized the black part –
and three times her eyes
were flat and grey in the distance
except when they were green and three
times the sweat curdled into teardrops
and we licked every sweatdrop up
together and laughed all the way to
the Million Man March

the way we love each other is not healthy
the therapist is a predator
the black boy knows this so doesn't want
to go there – the way we love each
other stifles bodies into wheezing
she does not know why he walks
so close to the sides of buildings
why he dresses like all the other black boys
why his pants sag why the hat
is pulled so low why he won't hang out
downtown all she knows is we wont
love right but the black boy fucks
like a champion

Elvis Presley
Justin Timberlake
Vanilla Ice
Michael Bolton
Kenny G
The White Rapper Reality Show

to tell a woman you don't love her
when you're both naked is inconveniently honest
not the place for it – if you are a black boy
it is the only place you can get away with
it shiny sweat pooling on your hip-bone
as you walk away from the rubble of
the bed

say black boy five times fast and he will appear
say inky binky spider
say the umbrella is just an accessory
say Steppin Fetchit was a legitimate actor
say America got it right once
say Tuskegee say Emmit Till
say Pine Ridge say Bay of Pigs
say Michael Jackson's blood is on all our hands

the boy became black at JFK
he does not know where he belongs anymore
he hears shouts of his tropical childhood
he listens for the sound of kite-tails in the wind
he is hip-hop he owns a green umbrella
he is resistance music and conflict diamonds
he is learning to love his scars he is making new
scars of his own –
they are beautiful – women flock
to the place where his downbeat sits
he is blacker than ever he is
blacker than ever   he is
blacker than ever

and he likes it

epilogue

Atonement

for Sean Thomas Dougherty

Dear Sean:

This morning at 8:30 on a crowded uptown 4 train, stuck in a tunnel because of a sick passenger up ahead, a woman gets interested in the cover of your book and asks, "what are you reading?" I say poetry. She says, "Read me one" and other passengers look at her funny, this done-up, corporate-type black woman who wants a poem on a crowded train on her way to work. I'm not sure what to do Sean. I don't want to disturb the other passengers, but then I think, these motherfuckers are fine when crackheads sing songs and beg them for change. I'm just reading a poem to a woman across the crowd. So I start with *Your Voice after Desnos,* and I get to the end and she says "That's it?!" I say "Yeah . . ." She says, "Read me another . . ." and the rest of the train is type uncomfortable, Sean. There are a couple smiles, some white women looking at her and frowning, a couple awkward away glances, but now there are also a couple folks taking out their iPod buds to check out the commotion, so I think, we have a good long stretch on a slow-ass uptown 4 train between 42nd and 125th, so I read *The Dark Soul of the Accordion.*

I start slow. Your first line is breathtaking, Sean. *My grandfather does not sleep among the roots . . .* and immediately everybody is hooked, everyone is in, the tattooed man whose name I imagine to be Gus, the elderly Phillipino men in the neat threadbare suits and dirty shoes, the Catholic school girl who's folded down the band of her skirt-waist so it can ride up over her thighs and this black woman with the corporate suit and satchel and muted red nail polish and immaculate hair—all of them are in, Sean and she is smiling like she won the lottery, and I'm reading your poem on the 4 train like it's mine, because I've already read it aloud to myself three times over the past two days, and the train, impossibly crowded; but I'm holding onto the center pole and dancing.

My friend Rupa, once told me I was kinetic, Sean; that I couldn't talk, let alone read a poem without the words pushing my most fervent prayers away from my ribcage, without looking like I was about to get up and run, and your poem is one I wish I could have written, so I'm reading it almost shouting now. I've got me some room around the center pole and I'm digging into the words, those taut lines like trenches: *my grandfather's eyes are rain across countless countries,* you say.

Sean, the train knows. It's picking up speed and starting to rumble past 59th and the train is more silent than every New Yorker's quiet memories of bodies flinging themselves like so many Icaruses from the center of that towering heat, all our unspoken fear, except for me; open and praying-chanting your poem now. The orchestra of the accordion's breath is my most verdant lung. I'm bobbing and weaving—me, your poem and 200 New Yorkers stuck in rush hour traffic on the uptown 4. It is the week between Rosh Hashanah and Yom Kippur. It is early Fall. I'm never up this early in the morning Sean, but I'm doing a class visit up at Fordham University, and I don't do these—early mornings—but I'm glad to be up and busy Sean, because it's work and I'm heartbroken. I hurt my girl Sean. I hurt her bad and I just want to not know how flawed I am every second of every moment, so I'm glad Sarah has offered me this visit. Sarah once recited, drunk out of her gourd, Psalm 100, to me and ten others in a bar over the jukebox which I imagine was playing Prince, but it could have been anything, and who knows if this has anything to do with this ride. I'm reading your poem past 86th, past 96th, me, the train, your grandfather's accordion—a single kinetic organism, and I hurt my girl and she's never coming back and I'm looking for any kind of redemption I can find, because I don't fully believe today that I'm a good man, and it's almost Kol Nidre and in your poem you ask your grandfather. *"Do you still consider yourself a Jew?"* and according to you, he doesn't even hesitate. He's on his deathbed. He's thought about this, and he says *"What is a Jew? If a Jew is someone who follows the Torah, no. But is that what makes a Jew? And if so, what good for others. what walls . . ."*

And it's 125th Street and there is applause and I almost forget to get off. I'm sweating and the corporate black woman is already gone and a couple folks nod, and one dude says "that was a pretty good way to spend a morning ride" and I get off and of course Sean, here's the kicker. None of this really happened, but it could Sean, it could. If I can see my way clear to read to a train full of people on Kol Nidre, I might be in the clear, but of course that's not exactly true either. A man can chase his own shadow for a long long time before he knows anything. Your grandfather knew this. In the end, he followed his mother's voice out of here. What irony. What poetry Sean. Your Poppa, a poet, the breath of an accordion, a socialist jester on his death bed. He is trying to free me on the 4 train. It's crowded and I'm reading silently but breathing like I'm running. I'm with you and your Poppa and I realize for a while my whole body is bending and nodding from the waist. The two schoolgirls are looking at me funny–kinetic. For a moment Sean, it feels like I'm davening.

Acknowledgments

All the journals and anthologies in which poems or earlier versions of poems within have appeared.

The best mother and brother on the planet, Hyacinth Bonair-Agard, Jamil Edward Agard, Lynne Procope and the LouderARTS Project, Volume Summer Institute and Jeff Kass, Vox Feris and Real Talk Avenue (Emily Rose, Baz, Laura–I see you!), YCA and Kevin Coval and the city of Chicago. All the young people who I teach; who teach me. Cave Canem where many of these poems were born. Queens Royal College and the 79to84 listserve which answers my questions and keeps the picong alive and reminds me that I really did see these things happen. Greg Pardlo for a good read and edit of the 'scrip. Angel Nafis, whose love and youthful wisdom trampolines many of these poems forward. Marty McConnell who had to put up with many of the very first drafts of these, and my general behavior in the interim. Geoff and Em forever. Maureen H. Benson. Patrick Rosal, who keeps me level, and disturbs the magic, and expands the worlds of these poems. Patricia Smith for pushing. Jeanann Verlee for trusting my work. My father, Roosevelt John Williams, my cousins Simi and Olufemi and the whole Ojurongbe / Oluwasanmi clan for finding me. Anthony Robert Perez, Anderson Thomas Perez–the beginning. Cleo Julien, for keeping Arouca massive in my heart . . . and in my belly. Larry Olton and family, for investing in his belief of me. Cyril Smith, who helped me bridge the difficult years. Central Synagogue New York City, for a whole other family and support; Barry Kugel and Gerda Leshin and Livia Thompson. Paola Prestini, Milica Paranosic and Vision Into Art whose commissions inspire much of the poems and push me as an artist. Jennifer, J.D. and the terranova collective. Of course Lisa Simmons, Willie Perdomo and Cypher Books. Kwame Dawes for the eagle eye and the always support and inspiration. Jeremy Poynting's close editing and Hannah Bannister at Peepal Tree Press. April Jones, whom I love, who is better than I.